COM
FC

A Metaphysical View

By Shepherd Hoodwin

Summerjoy Press
Laguna Niguel, California
2019

COMPASSION FOR EVIL
A Metaphysical View

Summerjoy Press
99 Pearl
Laguna Niguel CA 92677-4818

shoodwin@gmail.com
https://shepherdhoodwin.com

Copyright © 2019 by Shepherd Hoodwin

All rights reserved. No part of this publication may be reproduced, stored in a retrieval system, or transmitted, in any form or by any means, electronic, mechanical, photocopying, recording, or otherwise, without the prior written permission of the publisher, except by a reviewer, who may quote brief passages in a review.

ISBN: 9781653886289

Photograph of Shepherd Hoodwin by John Kilis.

CONTENTS

INTRODUCTION		v
1	FREE WILL	1
2	THE SOUL	2
3	ANGER AND FEAR	4
4	THE SURVIVAL INSTINCT	7
5	US VERSUS THEM	8
6	REVENGE	9
7	RELEASING ANGER AND FEAR	11
8	THE DIVINE SPARK	12
9	KARMA	14
10	THE VALUE OF ADVERSITY	18
11	THE MEANS CREATE THE END	20
12	THE FIELD OF LOVE	21
13	FEAR NO EVIL	23
14	ME AND MY SHADOWS	24
15	FORGIVENESS	26
16	TERRORIST OR FREEDOM-FIGHTER?	27
17	WHAT IS TRULY RIGHT?	29
18	THE MYTH OF BAD BOYS	31
19	PERPETRATORS	32
20	VICTIMS	33

21	CONSCIENCE AND GUILT	34
22	PEACE	35
23	ASTRAL SUICIDE	36
24	REDEMPTION	37
25	BELL CURVE	39
26	THE TREE OF THE KNOWLEDGE OF GOOD AND EVIL	42
	CONCLUSION	44
	ABOUT THE AUTHOR	45
	OTHER BOOKS BY SHEPHERD HOODWIN	47
	REVIEWS	52

INTRODUCTION

The Michael teachings are an extraordinary body of channeled material that paint a vivid portrait of how we, as eternal souls, set up our lifetimes—why we're here, what our lessons are, and how we can learn them more efficiently and joyfully.

I am a Michael channel. My site (below) links to several Michael books I've written. This short one explores the nature of evil from the soul's point of view, and how we can skillfully deal with it as lightworkers.

The genesis of this book was a channeling I did on the subject two decades ago. I knew then that I wanted to publish something on this topic, but it has proven to be a tough nut to crack. In 2010, a shorter version of it went out in my *Perspectives* newsletter. When I revisited it, I did a great deal more work on it, and this is the result.

I hope it helps you find greater peace in dealing with life on this challenging planet.

   Shepherd Hoodwin
   shepherdhoodwin@gmail.com
   https://shepherdhoodwin.com
   February 10, 2019

1 FREE WILL

Inherent in the physical plane school that each of us attends is free will, so that we are able to learn to choose and create. That makes for the possibility of evil—willfully harming others. From a higher point of view, that's not necessarily a "bad" thing because we can become more conscious of light by seeing it clearly against its absence, darkness. Polarity is an intrinsic part of our life's structure—we gain understanding by comparing and contrasting opposites. Learning what not to do can help bring into focus what to do, and why, expanding light. Genesis says that on the first day of creation, "God divided the light from the darkness." That also happens for souls here on the first plane of creation.

As with most things, there are positive and negative expressions of darkness. Darkness is a necessary half of creation—it provides raw material. For example, the darkness of the future gives us the possibility of creating new things. Evil is an example of negative darkness. Choosing to do evil is optional, but most people have willfully harmed others at some point, to some degree. Of course, there is a wide range of harm, from relatively petty, such as acting spitefully, to devastating, such as genocide. In both cases, there is malicious intent, but the scope is vastly different.

2   THE SOUL

There are many levels of self. Our core is what the Michael teachings call a *spark of the Tao*, which is a unit of consciousness of the All That Is. Religious people might call that "the God within." That part of self is mostly untouched by evil because it is not directly involved in polarity. It creates an *essence* that contains a blueprint for how we will manifest on the seven planes of creation of Earth—our potentialities. The outer layer of our essence is our *soul*, which animates and carries all our human lifetimes. It extends a part of itself into each body/mind, inhabiting it and giving it self-awareness. Animals also have souls, *hive* souls, which are simpler than human *sentient* souls because they are not designed to make reasoned choices; they have awareness, but not conscious self-awareness. Without a soul, a body would be vacant—nobody would be "home" other than the body's own instinctual consciousness.

Sentient souls, who learn through making choices, have varying degrees of negativity based on their choices over many lifetimes. There are some who could justifiably be classified as evil. They are those at the far end of the spectrum who have not only done a lot of evil acts but whose hearts have fully hardened, who are unreachable by love. They have no sense of connection with others or the whole—they are completely self-centered. There are few truly evil people, if we define them this way. Most souls who do numerous evil acts eventually prove to be capable of some redemption.

Nearly all of those whose hearts are profoundly hardened are younger souls who had many harsh experiences early in their incarnations and didn't properly get their bearings. It usually starts with their being victims of extreme abuse and not having the resources to rise above it. Instead, as part of their strategy to stay safe, they become stuck in a pattern of seeking power over others and exacting revenge. As they harm more and more people, they become overwhelmingly enmeshed in karma. Their heavy ego defenses keep them from recognizing their own culpability. Eventually, love may not be able to get through.

3 ANGER AND FEAR

To understand why people do seemingly senseless evil things, we need to understand anger and fear. They are two sides of one coin, not so much emotions but physically hardwired impulses that arise when we perceive threats to our survival. Anger is the instinct to push something away, and fear is the instinct to withdraw from it. They can be useful in the presence of real, imminent threats, mobilizing us to act. Anger is masculine (outgoing) and fear is feminine (incoming). Some people react more with anger, and some with fear, but behind anger is fear, and behind fear is anger—they are inseparable, like the male and female sides of the yin/yang symbol. It is easier to sympathize with people who are fearful than with those who are angry, because angry people can be prickly and dangerous, so it is helpful to recognize the fear behind anger.

Humanity could quickly evolve a great deal if we learned how to constructively deal with anger and fear. Certainly, that's an important part of the growth of anyone on a conscious spiritual path. We all have some stuck anger and fear in our subconscious stored when we were powerless to act on it, including during early childhood and past lives. Some of it doesn't belong to us: we all pick up energies from other people and from the mass consciousness. Releasing this backlog as

ANGER AND FEAR

much as possible can help us become happier—it is a heavy burden. Ideally, we would learn not to store them in the first place but instead release them when they arise and the opportunity to take constructive action passes. In the wild, many animals do this instinctively, such as shaking out stress after an encounter with a predator.

Like food, anger and fear spoil with age. The nature of energy is to move, and when it is stuck, it causes damage. Letting it fester and obsessing about "getting even" can destroy many lives, including our own. However, we are unconscious of much of our stored anger and fear, which can lead to many physical and mental health problems. Sometimes they erupt as an overreaction to current events that remind us of them and trigger us. That is an opportunity to become aware of them and heal.

We can only do that if we don't identify with them. A core meditation technique is to observe our thoughts and feelings and let them pass through us without attachment to them. There's a saying, "Don't believe everything you think." We might add, "and feel." This non-attachment is a key to spiritual awakening. Ultimately, only love, truth, and beauty are real; all the rest is illusion, if sometimes quite convincing. If we recognize what isn't in harmony with them as things needing to be healed and evolved, we can neutralize our stored anger and fear. Those who do evil identify with and justify them rather than observing them from a higher vantage point. They invest so much energy in trying to preserve their physical body that they cannot perceive themselves as being anything more than that, let alone an eternal soul.

Anyone who seeks healing can find it, but those who deliberately harm others are probably not yet at the point of seeking it; they may not know yet that they need healing or that it is even possible. Maybe they don't have a vision of another way to be. They also likely don't have tools to deal with the intensely compressed energies seething within them.

4 THE SURVIVAL INSTINCT

Anger and fear mostly originate in the body's survival instinct. If we didn't have a survival instinct, it would be too easy to walk off cliffs. The human animal we each inhabit is hardwired to blindly do whatever seems necessary to survive, on autopilot, without thinking. We rarely make the best possible choices on autopilot—it provides crude, "one size fits all" solutions. A main reason we incarnate into these bodies is to learn to blend soul with animal, to unite "heaven and earth." That brings "adult supervision." The more we advance spiritually, the more we navigate our instincts with skill, like a master rider on a spirited horse. We apply reason and loving wisdom to our choices. We neither repress nor express our anger and fear, but instead view them as useful information that we can act on in the most constructive way.

5 US VERSUS THEM

Our survival instinct guards against strangers and is suspicious of the "other." This is where the us-versus-them paradigm that fuels so much evil comes from. Hunter/gatherers lived in small clans and didn't know if those who lived beyond the clan's control meant ill. Some of that caution remains useful, but once the facts are ascertained and new people are vetted, it makes sense to let it go. However, those with stuck, excess fear don't easily allow in new information, leading to the xenophobia (irrational dislike or fear of people from other countries) so common today. Politicians exploit that fear to get people to follow them.

The viciousness that can be exhibited by predatory animals is sometimes used to excuse human evil and an "every man for himself" ethos. However, wild animals aren't necessarily a good role model for humans, who have the intellectual capacity to make reasoned choices. Animals have no choice but to act out of their survival instincts when they feel threatened; we do. Furthermore, the internet is full of videos of animals lovingly playing together who might have been enemies in the wild. If they can do it, certainly we can.

6 REVENGE

The desire for revenge is also part of our survival instinct. In the primitive world, revenge kept people in line to some extent—they knew that there could be dire consequences for bad behavior—although even then it didn't work very well. Revenge tends to trap people in endless cycles of retaliation, making things worse, because they often don't acknowledge their own culpability. They don't see the relationship between what someone just did to them and what they did earlier.

This is a song lyric I wrote. It can be heard at https://shepherdhoodwin.com/about-shepherd/songs-by-shepherd/

The History of the World

Long ago,
Long ago,
Someone
Did something to someone else, who
Did something to someone else, who
Did something to someone else, who
Did something to someone else, who
Did something to someone else, who
Did something to someone else, who
Says revenge is sweet?

COMPASSION FOR EVIL

Part of the development of human civilization has been the attempt to control the impulse for revenge, which can create chaos. The idea of "an eye for an eye" was originally a step forward, designed to keep revenge-seekers from taking more than an eye (for example, murdering). Then, Jesus taught that even that was obsolete and suggested turning the other cheek. Exactly what that looks like has been debated, and even today, few do more than pay lip service to it, but it is about meeting hate with love. In the same passage, he suggested that we love our enemies, which precludes seeking vengeance. "Vengeance is mine…saith the Lord"—in other words, karma, the natural way the universe balances energy, will take care of it.

Those who live from love obviously don't need a fear of retribution to keep them from doing harm, but most people need to know that boundaries will be enforced. When the rule of law is reasonably just and consistent, it helps maintain order, allowing civilization to develop. It discourages people from taking matters into their own hands, possibly doling out punishment far out of proportion to the crime. Some legal form of redress can help satisfy our sense of justice. Unfortunately, legal retribution is rarely concerned with rehabili-tation; the intent is punitive rather than healing. Therefore, many criminals commit more crimes after getting out of prison.

7 RELEASING ANGER AND FEAR

For those who wish to get off the karmic wheel, there is no substitute for letting go of things we cannot do anything about, but that can be challenging. There are many excellent healing modalities that can help us. We can therapeutically release anger without harm using methods such as hitting pillows or pounding the water while swimming. A more advanced, less draining approach is to meditate and feel the anger until it burns off, simply witnessing it. EFT (Emotional Freedom Technique: https://www.eftuniverse.com) and TAT (Tapas Acupressure Technique: https://tatlife.com) can also be used; they instruct the nervous system to release charges of various kinds. The key factor is our intent to let go. In learning to deal wisely with evil impulses within ourselves, we become better equipped to deal with evil outside ourselves.

8 THE DIVINE SPARK

Everything in the universe is built from love, truth, and beauty. Even those who are evil have a divine spark within them; they have just cut themselves off from it due to being extremely damaged, limited, and unevolved. Compassion sees the damage rather than just dismissing them, at the same time protecting self and others from them.

This divine spark is why some people argue that evil doesn't really exist, that all people are good inside, although they acknowledge that there is much ignorance and immaturity. Of course, with words it's a matter of how we define and understand them. Willfully harming others certainly occurs, whatever we call it. Souls *can* become damaged and stuck on the way to evolving. Still, the word *evil* should probably be used sparingly. Casually accusing others of being evil is polarizing, fostering an us-versus-them mentality, and doesn't aid constructive discussion.

Nevertheless, the way to avoid dualistic thinking is not by denying that evil exists but by being compassionate and nonjudgmental toward those who do evil. Being nonjudgmental isn't saying that harmful behavior is permissible. We can condemn violating behavior while refusing to see those who violate as being less than human—

monsters or mustache-twirling bad guys—or subscribing to the illusion that we're separate or intrinsically different from each other. The very fact that those who do evil see their victims as being less than human is what allows them to do evil, so seeing evil people as themselves being less than human does not help matters. They may behave monstrously, but there are reasons for it. They have feelings, even if they are completely cut off from them. We all partake of the same human condition and deal with fundamentally the same issues. Honesty requires that we acknowledge that we each have within us some unresolved anger and fear that can lead to doing harm when we don't choose love.

9 KARMA

It's helpful to understand evil within the larger context of how souls evolve through having experiences. One of the most growthful, if painful, kinds of experience is incurring and repaying karma. It's the core curriculum of the School of Hard Knocks. It's also possible to study at the School of Joy, but most of us start out, at least, as students at Hard Knocks U. Especially during younger soul ages, people can become bored without some karma to stir things up, and may seek it out.

When harm to others is great enough that their right to choose is significantly abridged and their ability to follow their path is diminished, it forms a major karmic debt, which is an energetic imbalance between two souls. Karmic harm is tangible. Simply hurting people's feelings or failing to meet their expectations is not karmic. Choosing what is within one's right to choose is not karmic. The Michael teachings do define a form of karma called "mind fuck," in which a person deliberately disrupts someone's sanity, but that interferes with his ability to lead his physical life. Psychic attack can also be karmic if it is severe enough and leads to tangible harm. Karma is basically taking energy that belongs to someone else that wants to return to its proper owner, like pulling a rubber band tacked to a hard surface.

No one has to decide whether an act is karmic or determine what the nature of the karma is—it is ingrained in the energy. When it is repaid, the energy becomes neutral—the charge goes flat—and the karmic bond is dissolved. There are various ways karmic debts can be repaid, some more positive than others. This can be negotiated beforehand on a soul level, but often repayment occurs in the heat of the moment, without planning, when those with a karmic bond meet—the energy rushes to balance itself.

Major karma must be repaid to the soul who suffered it. There are also lesser karmas. Intermediate karma, which inflicts a temporary setback that is not life-altering, can be repaid to the soul who suffered it but doesn't have to be. Minor karma, such as mean words, do not have to be repaid to an individual at all but tend to color the overall energy of one's life and attract similar treatment. "What goes around comes around."

We are all responsible for our actions, but karmic implications are tempered by the motivations behind them; for example, a murder committed under the influence or in self-defense usually has a different, less grievous karmic imprint than one committed in cold blood. The principle "like attracts like" applies to karma. A foot soldier killing another soldier in a war, inflicting no more harm than is required by societally accepted conventions, may not incur a karmic debt at all.

Not all karmic acts have an evil (malicious) intent. Sometimes they are done out of ignorance or are sincerely seen at the time as being necessary or even helpful. Many karmic acts, however, are deliberately cruel and violating.

Over our many lifetimes, we've all been on both sides of various kinds of karma, caught up in the heat of the moment or doggedly marching on in blind ignorance. We often form karma because we had previously been scalded by trauma or overwhelmed with challenges beyond our abilities to handle, but sometimes we just don't know better. It is natural to have particular compassion for victims, but if we look further back, perpetrators often were also victims. Having compassion and understanding for all of us can help us get off the karmic wheel, the repetitive cycle of victimization and perpetration.

Souls must repay all major karmic debts before completing the physical plane; otherwise, they would keep feeling pulled back. Ideally, they finally put two and two together and realize that they have done to others what others have done to them, that they are both victim and perpetrator. They learn to receive their karmic repayments with some grace, at least without retaliation that would form new karmic ribbons. Some even enroll in the School of Joy.

A number of souls, however, graduate the physical plane with a C average. They tire of the karmic wheel, do the minimum to pay their debts and move on without much self-awareness. They remain students of the School of Hard Knocks until the end. Michael (the entity I channel) is fond of saying, "All is choice." No one figuratively puts a gun to a soul's head to force them to face themselves, acknowledge their errors, and open to unconditional love. We all have at least one spirit guide in every lifetime (and we are often guides to others between lifetimes). Like tutors in school, our guides encourage us to grow, and do their best to help us. Most souls make at least some progress throughout their lifetimes. However, what we do remains our choice.

10 THE VALUE OF ADVERSITY

A main reason that souls incarnate is to evolve, however that occurs. In this regard, evil can be useful. Like all adversity, evil is a teacher: it tests what we know and shows us where we still need work. Without it, we would probably grow less. (Note the similarity of the words *evil* and *evolve*.) Although unwelcome at the time, we sometimes look back on harsh experiences with gratitude, seeing that we became more fully realized as a result of them. Sometimes, we are not merely broken but broken open.

Michael emphasizes that we need not grow this way—we can choose to grow through joy. According to them, the average percentage of negativity for humanity is 48%. There are sentient (self-aware) beings on other planets with far less evil and negativity in general. Their growth is generally slower but more pleasant, with relatively little drama. Human beings are the drama queens of the universe. ☺ There are pros and cons to just about everything. One of the pros of all this drama is that it can result in a deeper emotional well, ultimately increasing our capacity for joy. Many sentient species have relatively subdued emotions. However, a con is that much human growth comes through pain, making life harder for us. In fact, human beings have taken destructiveness to unspeakable extremes (partly due to the hardwired aggressiveness of the human animal). No decent person can fail to be horrified by the atrocities humans commit. It is possible to develop rich emotions without going to such extremes.

Some people believe that people like Hitler agreed on a soul level to sacrifice themselves and did humanity a great service by playing the roles they did, showing us something about ourselves. It *can* lead to evolution when the dark corners of the human psyche are reflected back to us on a large screen. Their actions shocked humanity, leading to growth in those willing to learn. However, they didn't do that out of the goodness of their hearts—that is built in to the growth-through-pain model: people in the "waking sleep" go to increasing extremes until they ram into a wall, hopefully waking up. If they don't, they go to the opposite extreme until they ram into *that* wall, ad nauseum. People who represent evil to the masses are simply playing out their beliefs to their logical conclusions. If they were good, they would have acted good, with kindness and integrity.

11 THE MEANS CREATE THE END

Imposing on others "for their own good" often rationalizes evil. A mark of evil is the attitude that the end justifies the means, but cruelty never serves a higher good. In fact, the means create the end. Evil means create evil ends.

Some fundamentalist Christians believe that an anti-Christ is coming who will disguise himself by seeming like a really good person. It's true that a nice person isn't necessarily good, although a good person will also probably be nice. But Jesus taught "By their fruits you shall know them." A good person has goodwill and helps others; an evil person has malice and hurts others—it's not rocket science. The majority of people have elements of both, and some straddle the middle. With enough observation, though, it's not hard for an unbiased, decent person to perceive whether someone has basic goodwill. Using dogma rather than common sense, fundamentalists can paint anyone they disagree with as evil. The truly good prioritize truth and fairness.

12 THE FIELD OF LOVE

The battle of good versus evil does not take place on the field of love. Those who see themselves as battling evil are playing on the field of karma, just like those they perceive as being evil. Love does not battle evil. It may act to contain it when necessary, but love does not battle at all—it illuminates. When there is enough light, darkness disappears.

It is sometimes necessary to take strong action to prevent aggression, such as through police or military action. However, even that can be done with compassion and restraint, not harming any more than is necessary. When police kill someone who could easily have been stopped in a less violent manner, they are usually overreacting due to unhealed anger and fear. People with major anger issues are sometimes attracted to work in law enforcement or the military because they seek license to vent their anger. It would be smart if such people were screened out through psychological testing.

After a conflict, a compassionate approach can help both perpetrators and victims heal. South Africa's Truth and Reconciliation Commission is an example. This can break the karmic circle and limit the continuation of ill will.

Perpetrators often feel that they are just reacting to previous injustices. Their grievances also need to be heard, whether or not they are valid. Sometimes, that can open the way to their realizing what their anger and fear are really about.

Love is not a doormat, but it isn't harsh, either. Love takes no pleasure in the use of force against others. Being cruelly punitive does not reduce the evil in the world. On the contrary, it increases it; it keeps everyone in the vicious circle of retaliation, in which we react to harm by creating more harm. If we want a better world, we need to shift to a higher paradigm that recognizes our unity.

13 FEAR NO EVIL

Carl Jung said, "What you resist not only persists, but grows." So Jesus's instruction to "Resist not evil" makes sense and applies to evil both in others and within ourselves. Chronically fearing or fighting evil keeps it alive, feeding and attracting negativity. It's more useful to cultivate at least neutrality, if not compassion, at the same time recognizing and practicing the powers we have to keep ourselves safe. That includes using common sense, such as not leaving our doors unlocked or walking alone at night in an unsafe place. Evil should be handled with care, but is not as powerful as it's generally thought to be. If others do harm us, our knowledge that we're eternal beings helps put it in perspective—we have less to lose. As souls, we know that Earth is a difficult planet and expect some scathing experiences, although we can learn to keep them to a minimum. Our human lives are valuable and worth protecting, but we cannot truly lose who we are and what we love.

14 ME AND MY SHADOWS

When we know our oneness with all beings, we cannot do harm. Evil can only exist in the us-versus-them paradigm. Those who subscribe to it use it to demonize others and project their shadows (what they don't want to see about themselves) onto them. "We're the good people, and (fill in the blank) are the evil ones." People on opposing sides often accuse each other of the same things. We can see this between conservatives and progressives. In our lack of self-awareness, we frequently see the fault in our conflicts as being totally someone else's; few of us acknowledge our own responsibility. Taking responsibility is a prerequisite to awakening. There are instances that are one-sided, but most aren't entirely, at least. With such pervasive ego defenses, it is hard to move forward. Exploring our shadows is one of the most growthful things we can undertake.

Those with compassion for evil are more likely to feel sadness and dismay about evil acts than vein-popping apoplexy and outrage, which result from being triggered. We are triggered by what appears similar to something unresolved and unhealed within ourselves, or its polar opposite (which is also similar). The parts of our ego protecting our shadows spring into action.

When we feel hurt, we often want our friends to agree that the offender is completely at fault and maybe a terrible person. We may feel annoyed if they try to understand the other person's point of view. One way we can create a more peaceful world is instead to ask our friends to simply support us and hear us compassionately. When we are ready, they may be able to help us explore what we can learn from the experience, including what our part in it may have been and the other person's perspective. Forgiveness, which releases negativity, is possible without understanding, but true understanding automatically brings forgiveness and goes beyond it. Working to understand why people did what they did can help us let go.

15 FORGIVENESS

There has been disagreement among survivors of horrors such as the Holocaust about whether to forgive. As with most such discussions, how you define *forgiveness* can determine your opinion. It doesn't mean that you let perpetrators off the hook or forget their actions. It simply means that you release your frozen energies around the event and initiate healing for all.

The ultimate goal for all souls is to learn unconditional love. Most do not completely reach it, but at least make progress toward it. Forgiveness is an essential step. Forgiving those who have severely violated us is difficult, but if we can do that, we have a skill that will accelerate our growth.

16 TERRORIST OR FREEDOM-FIGHTER?

Reality is at least three-dimensional, and people are complicated and changeable. A two-dimensional cartoon devil ("d" plus *evil*) is a childish conception. There are few hand-rubbing villains who think of themselves as being evil. Most people playing in the karmic field see themselves as the good guys. George Washington thought of himself as fighting tyranny, doing what he had to do, but the British saw him as a terrorist. Many we view today as terrorists no doubt think of themselves as freedom-fighters, too. Most of us believe that we're in the right most of the time, even if we're not. We need to find common ground and respectful, if imperfect, ways to resolve disputes if humanity is to survive. The most righteous solutions won't always win the day. We all have blind spots that can make it difficult to see what is truly right, but with some goodwill and give-and-take on all sides, we can at least move forward without destroying ourselves.

In many cases, terrorists such as suicide bombers had been told that they were making a noble sacrifice that would be rewarded in heaven. Their peers may have considered them to be really good people. Mediums who communicate with the other side (the astral plane) have seen their extreme disillusionment once passing over. They feel the heavy weight of the karma they created, not the promised paradise. As is so often the case, the problem is that they were given wrong information, "fake news." Having an accurate understanding of karma and how the universe works is invaluable for those pursuing a spiritual path.

There is such a thing as "necessary evils." Many wars are pointless and unnecessary, and could have been avoided with some compassionate and skillful handling of earlier disagreements. Still, there are power-hungry leaders who invade other countries. Sometimes, a war to stop an aggressor is the lessor of two evils. A person oriented in love does not mistake that for good. A truly good person regrets the necessity rather than gloating over victory. Everyone who dies in war was someone's father, mother, sister, brother, or friend. We are all eternal beings, including those who do evil. We are all part of the same grand experiment in expanding love's understanding of itself.

17 WHAT IS TRULY RIGHT?

Usually, both sides believe themselves to be right and the other, wrong. The reality frequently is that there are both right and wrong on both sides to some degree. When we are caught up in defending our position, it is difficult to see the right in the other side. If we are willing to honestly examine our own motivations and respect that our opponents may have valid points, we can begin to have clarity about what is truly right and wrong. In general, the more work we've done on our own shadows and stored anger and fear, and the more we are acquainted with love, truth, and beauty, the easier it is to perceive what is in alignment with them. It becomes impossible to abuse others and claim that it's done out of love, for example, because we know that love isn't abusive, and we know what love feels like versus abuse.

1 Corinthians 13:4-7:

> Love is patient, love is kind. It does not envy, it does not boast, it is not proud. It does not dishonor others, it is not self-seeking, it is not easily angered, it keeps no record of wrongs. Love does not delight in evil but rejoices with the truth. It always protects, always trusts, always hopes, always perseveres.

If you are a judge, jury member, or another third party sorting out a dispute, the same principles apply: Having as much internal clarity as possible so that your own issues aren't triggered will help you make the best decision. Of course, there is also the matter of sorting out and verifying the facts, and having the ability to reason well. But high integrity and a strong sense of fairness are essential.

18 THE MYTH OF BAD BOYS

Evil people are often thought of as getting away with things and having more fun. However, karma is a heavy weight to bear; there is a built-in incentive to pay it back because it feels so bad. Those who have done much harm to others live in a self-created hell. They may gratify their appetites freely, but they do it in order to further dull their feelings. They live in denial in order to cope. There can be no real joy in such a state.

Almost anything can become an addiction, and certain "adrenalin junkies" become addicted to the "thrill" of violating others and breaking rules, flaunting being caught. It relieves the boredom of their chronically dulled senses. Others are simply addicted to having power over others, compensating for a deep underlying sense of powerlessness. Secure people have no need for power over others except to ensure everyone's freedom.

Furthermore, energy "vampires" can feed off the life force that is released when someone dies suddenly; murdering can be like cracking open an egg, letting *chi* escape that the murderer can take in. More advanced souls know that they can tap into the unlimited supply of energy within, but many people still seek it outside themselves.

19 PERPETRATORS

Having compassion for perpetrators is not easy to do, but it is well worth the effort—hating perpetrators increases our own negativity and brings us down. As with addicts, those who do evil could be seen as having an illness, their actions a sort of insanity, even when they go about them in a cold, calculated way. That only indicates that their insanity has hardened.

20 VICTIMS

Some believe that everything is self-created and that there is no such thing as victims. However, the universe is half order/half chaos. With free will, individuals can choose to harm others.

We may attract negative treatment because of our karma or beliefs (self-karma). It is especially instructive to explore repetitive patterns. When the same issues keep arising, we can be sure that we are somehow creating them from dysfunctional beliefs in our subconscious—we are the common denominator in those events.

Sometimes, though, we just happen to be in the wrong place at the wrong time. To believe that we create everything is to believe that we can fully control other people's actions, which is clearly not the case. When someone forms karma with us, we are technically a victim, by definition. We can choose to frame it as a growth opportunity, which it is, albeit a painful one. Karma is part of the lessons of the physical plane. It often takes us by surprise and challenges us in new ways.

21   CONSCIENCE AND GUILT

Sensitive people who struggle with inner demons may think of themselves as being worse off than those without conscience, but in moving forward with integrity, there is light at the end of the tunnel, and joy becomes increasingly available. Only integrity lets us align with our true self. Those without conscience have no chance of experiencing joy.

Ironically, those plagued by guilt, deserved or otherwise, have much less to be concerned about than sociopaths without a capacity for it, because at least they care, rather than simply rationalizing their harm to others. Guilt communicates to us that we need to examine ourselves. However, guilt can feed ego, too; when it dominates, it can paralyze us and stand in the way of actually rectifying our mistakes, if they truly were mistakes, and letting go if they were not.

As we learn to do the right thing every time, simply because it is the right thing, to the best of our ability, life becomes simpler and guilt becomes less of an issue. Evil manipulates others to try to get desired results; good does the right thing and lets the results take care of themselves.

22 PEACE

We can learn to avoid karma and other negativity, especially as we lose our fascination with heavy drama and instead truly love peace. We also avoid trouble more often when we listen to our intuition and spiritual guidance.

The television and movie dramas that people are drawn to, and the music people listen to, are often filled with gratuitous violence. People give lip service to wanting peace but frequently make choices that lead to the opposite. It makes one question how much they really want peace. If humanity actually wanted peace, we'd have it. It's fine for everyone to be wherever they are in their soul development, and to enjoy whatever entertainment they like. Again, all choices can contribute to growth—it's all good, as they say—and some souls have a greater need for excitement. When we are ready for peace, however, our choices reflect that—they contribute to peace internally and externally.

23 ASTRAL SUICIDE

Evil is both destructive and self-destructive. The rare soul that cannot find its way out of hardened evil, lifetime after lifetime, eventually self-destructs. Not all souls complete the physical plane and continue on; a few return to light by disassembling rather than by evolving, when there is no hope of it. It's like flunking out of school. Their soul substance breaks down into its components rather than returning to the Tao as a distinct being.

24 REDEMPTION

Anyone with remorse, however, who wants to find a way out, can eventually break through to an ability to feel at least somewhat connected to the whole and act more harmoniously with it, which are characteristics of goodness. Some souls remain a highly mixed bag even until the end of their cycle of human lifetimes—they are the ones who graduate with a C average—so perfection is not required.

Those who break through profoundly can bring great gifts both to self and to humanity. Referring to highly destructive leaders, I channeled Michael as saying:

> A person who plays upon the larger stage of human drama represents all the people who feed into him. Those who give him his power are tied to him energetically. His growth, however it may come, can be their growth, to some extent, and their growth can be his. Therefore, anyone who wakes up, who was blind but begins to see beyond a negative collective consciousness, can empower others to do the same more quickly than would have been the case on their own. No experience is wasted, because when learning results from it, it can help all those who participated in it to evolve.

COMPASSION FOR EVIL

It is a paradox that good can ultimately come out of evil. When souls have been enmeshed in the dark but finally come to the light, they appreciate the light more than they would have had their path been easier, and have knowledge they cannot lose. They are inoculated against the patterns they perpetuated when they were in darkness. They have a sense of how precious love is, and what hell it is to live in the absence of that, which is what evil is—the absence of love, a partial void.

That brings to mind the hymn "Amazing Grace":

I once was lost, but now am found,
Was blind, but now I see.
'Twas grace that taught my heart to fear,
And grace my fears relieved.

25 BELL CURVE

Most of us carry both good and evil within us to some extent. Simplistically, we could think of it as a bell curve in which, say, five percent of the population are consistently altruistic, five percent are consistently ruthless, and the rest are somewhere in the middle. Even among the consistently ruthless, most still have a glimmer of humanity (Hitler loved dogs); even among the consistently altruistic, almost all still struggle with some negativity—it's part of the human condition.

Although we as souls vibrate at a certain place on this spectrum, on average, it is hard to evaluate where anyone is on it, especially when our biases are activated and we don't know the whole of the person. Therefore, it's a good idea to give others (and ourselves) the benefit of the doubt and not be too quick to assume we know where they are. Each of us is more evolved in some areas than in others. Some of us swing to extremes, especially those who haven't faced their shadows, whereas others are more consistent. If someone's energy currently feels dark and unpleasant, that could be a temporary state, for various reasons.

We are much larger than our current incarnation. People's personalities often don't reflect their true soul nature—they can choose to cut themselves off from it. A loving soul's outer energy can temporarily degrade due to various factors such as illness or circumstance. Those under the influence of alcohol or drugs or who are mentally ill may act more negatively than they normally would; repressed darkness that may not accurately represent the whole person may take over, in a given moment or even a given lifetime. Some manifestations of evil are due to problems that are more on the surface, such as a chemical imbalance due to toxins, whereas others reflect deeper, more problematic issues carried over several lifetimes, such as PTSD from having been tortured and murdered.

Advanced souls are better able to continue to make positive choices even when suffering physically, mentally, emotionally, or energetically. That is a skill well worth practicing. Most of us, however, don't consistently do that. For example, many of us become cranky when we don't feel well or are tired, and sometimes lash out.

There can also be increased negativity temporarily from foreign entities such as parasitic lower astral plane energies that enter through a person's wounds. They can exaggerate his or her negative behavior and make it harder to change course. Like attracts like: negative entities are drawn to human negativity and feed off of it. Once embedded, they try to increase it so that they have more food. Removing them is often an important step in spiritual healing.

BELL CURVE

In addition to people who appear to be more negative than they truly are as souls, the opposite can also be true: a soul may, on average, vibrate closer to the evil end of the spectrum but currently be manifesting innocuously.

If our aim is to have unconditional love and respect for all beings, including compassion for evil, it doesn't much matter exactly where a soul is on the spectrum, since every experience can be used for growth. All we need to do is deal skillfully with whatever behavior is in front of us. Still, it can be useful to understand what challenges others are dealing with, where they are in their spiritual development, which is much more than just what the Michael teachings refer to as soul age (our five stages of growth on the physical plane).

Unconditional love doesn't imply that we feel equally connected to everyone, or even that we like or would choose to spend time with everyone. We naturally resonate with some more than others. It does imply that we keep an open mind about others and do not tear them down; we support their own journey toward greater love, wherever they are on the bell curve, wherever possible.

26 THE TREE OF THE KNOWLEDGE OF GOOD AND EVIL

People can have vastly different ideas about what constitutes good and evil actions. Some fundamentalist religions believe, for instance, that dancing on Sundays or using contraception is evil. The only valid measure of evil is the actual tangible harm it does, which doesn't include affronting someone's conditioned beliefs. Evil, like karma, trespasses on others.

Genesis 2:17:

> But of the tree of the knowledge of good and evil, thou shalt not eat of it: for in the day that thou eatest thereof thou shalt surely die.

That refers, in part, to being judgmental, making arbitrary rules that harden into dogma about what is good and evil. When we do that, we become constricted, no longer free to live authentically according to our eternal nature, and hence we die. We try to play God by seeking to enforce our self-created rules, exacting vengeance when others violate them. If we want to eat of the tree of life, we respect that if people truly create karma, they will repay it one way or another without our interference. We mind our own business, and live and let live. It is necessary and proper for governments to enact laws to

THE TREE OF THE KNOWLEDGE OF GOOD AND EVIL

penalize obvious infringements, such as murder and theft—civilizations cannot progress without them—but interference in the choices that are an individual's right to make is not "good work," as Michael calls it.

This verse also refers to reacting to the results of others' choices (eating of the fruits), whether perceived as good or evil, becoming entangled in them. To eat of the tree of life, we live from the inside out rather than the outside in. We make each choice consciously in the moment rather than having knee-jerk reactions to others. We act cleanly, with integrity, from our core.

CONCLUSION

Looking for people's humanity, even when it seems scarce, can help reinforce it, whereas engaging with negativity reinforces that. At the same time, it's smart to be realistic about the limitations of the people we deal with. If they are not open, nothing we say or do will likely have much immediate effect, although wise words and/or a positive example may plant a seed for the future.

We never know what the result of loving unconditionally will be. However, we don't do it for a result, but simply to be aligned with love. We have compassion for those who do evil not because of who they are but because of who we are. Increasing the vibration of love in humanity is the only way it can be healed.

Humanity has taken itself to the brink of total destruction. In our era, we have the opportunity to shift onto an easier path of growth. We do that first by facing ourselves fully with love, both the good and evil, the evolved and unevolved. Healing and integrating our shadows allow us to discover our true nature of love, truth, and beauty. Then we can offer that to others.

We're all in this together. With compassion for all, we can be a source of healing, helping find true solutions and bringing darkness to light.

ABOUT THE AUTHOR

SHEPHERD HOODWIN has been channeling since 1986. He also does intuitive readings, mediumship, past-life regression, healing, counseling, and channeling coaching (teaching others to channel). He has conducted workshops on the Michael teachings throughout the United States and Europe.

Shepherd is a graduate of the University of Oregon. He lives in Laguna Niguel, California.

https://shepherdhoodwin.com

TWITTER:
@shepherdh
@EnlightenNitwit

FACEBOOK:
https://www.facebook.com/shepherd.hoodwin
https://www.facebook.com/shepherd.hoodwin.author/
https://www.facebook.com/JourneyOfYourSoul/
https://www.facebook.com/EnlightenmentforNitwits/

shepherdhoodwin@gmail.com

Summerjoy Press
99 Pearl
Laguna Niguel CA 92677-4818

OTHER BOOKS BY SHEPHERD HOODWIN

Available at https://shepherdhoodwin.com/book/

All Is Choice

Few realize how profound, multi-faceted, and far-reaching the concept of choice is in our spiritual growth. This short book explores topics such as what is and is not our right to choose, our power as creators and the limits of our reality creation, how consciousness expands, and much more.

Being in the World

This insightful book explores practical spirituality.

Embracing What Is
Spiritual Keys to Happiness

This book is an abridged version of *Happiness and the Michael Teachings*, without technical Michael teachings terminology. A free version is available at Smashwords.com.

Energy Literacy
How to Perceive and Take Charge of Your Spiritual Well-Being

Energy Literacy is a short introduction to how to perceive our energy field and release negativity.

Topics include chakras, contracts, vows, cording, entities, implants, psychic attack, earthbound souls, soul retrieval, and more.

Enlightenment for Nitwits
The Complete Guide

This hilarious metaphysical/self-help humor collection will appeal to Oprah and Dave Barry fans as well as those with more esoteric interests. In a style reminiscent of comedian Steven Wright, it's full of wry one-liners along with longer, hilariously mind-bending pieces on a wide range of subjects, tied together by the idea of clueless humans trying to find enlightenment.

"I love *Enlightenment for Nitwits*! It is the funniest book I have read in several decades. If laughter leads to enlightenment, it will certainly do it. Nothing—thank God—is sacred in this delightful spoof on life in general."
—C. Norman Shealy, M.D., author of *Life Beyond 100*

Growing Through Joy

This thought-provoking book explores the nature of personal growth.

Happiness and the Michael Teachings
Learning to Embrace What Is

Happiness is the ultimate goal of every spiritual teaching. Here we explore several principles of what the Michael teachings refer to as growing through joy.

Healing the Gut
A Crib Sheet for Eliminating SIBO

This short ebook offers tips for those with digestive problems and related diseases, focusing on the Specific Carbohydrate Diet.

Journey of Your Soul
A Channel Explores the Michael Teachings

This is the most in-depth discussion of the Michael teachings to date. It may also be the first analytical study of channeling written by a channel. It has forewords by John Friedlander, author of *Psychic Psychology*, and Jon Klimo, author of *Channeling: Investigations on Receiving Information from Paranormal Sources*. Klimo writes, "*Journey of Your Soul* may well be the best (Michael) book of them all due to its clarity, thoroughness, and detail, and thanks to the fact that the author, an exceptionally clear-headed Michael channel himself, brings real integrity and authenticity to our understanding of Michael in particular and to the channeling process in general."

Loving from Your Soul
Creating Powerful Relationships

This inspiring, transformative book explores the nature of love itself as well as practical matters of relationships. One reader wrote, "There are phrases that are so inspiring that I wrote them down to refer to when I need them. I am looking forward to reading this book again and again."

Meditations for Self-Discovery
Guided Journeys for Communicating with Your Inner Self

This is a beautiful collection of forty-five vivid, often pastoral, guided imagery meditations channeled from Shepherd's essence. There are many meditation recordings available, but this is one of the first collections of meditations in book form that can be read to oneself or others. Teachers and group leaders would find it particularly useful.

Opening to Healing

This uplifting book explores the spiritual aspect of healing.

Unconditional Love in Politics
Or Have You Hugged a Republican/Democrat Today?

Is unconditional love in politics an oxymoron? Thus far, it's been a rare commodity if it's ever been there. This book explores what you can do about it, as well as why both right and left have useful parts to play in our evolution, the factors that influence a person's tilt to the right or left, and what unconditional love might look like in this sphere.

Why We're Attracted
Spiritual, Psychological and Physical Elements That Draw Us to Others

Just why are we attracted to some people and not to others? This book explores a multitude of factors on three levels: spiritual, psychological, and physical. Topics include agreements, life path, soul chemistry, male/female energy ratio, celibacy, body-type attraction, sexual orientation, monogamy, and polyfidelity.

REVIEWS

Excellent!

A must read to help expand one's understanding of oneself.

Thank you articulating these concepts so beautifully.
   I've sent my twenty-three-year-old son many excerpts to help him move more calmly through this time of transition into the real world.

A great book to help understand the shadows and light that are part of all of us. I highly recommend this to those seeking to expand their perspective on some important and interesting aspects of human nature.

Helped me a great deal.

We read this to one another last night. Excellent and so much to process. I will be rereading this for sure.

The author has such a fluid way of writing and sweet control of the language that everything flows naturally and beautifully.

REVIEWS

As expected, I learned a lot. I'm sure I will read it again and again. Something tells me that each time, I will be enlightened over and over.

Loved it! Bravo.

Printed in Great Britain
by Amazon